HEALING
FROM
PERSONAL
TRAUMAS:
New Beginnings

ISBN: 978-1-954341-29-6 (Paperback)

The views expressed in this book are solely those of the author and do not necessarily reflect the views of the publisher, and the publisher hereby disclaims any responsibility for them.

BRANDING

Writers' Branding
1800-608-6550
www.writersbranding.com
orders@writersbranding.com

CONTENTS

Dedication   i

Introduction   iii

Chapter 1 Childhood Trauma   1

Chapter 2 Teenage Trauma   5

Chapter 3 Adult Trauma   9

Chapter 4 Marital Years of Trauma   13

Chapter 5 Healing Years   23

Chapter 6 New Beginnings   35

Chapter 7 From Caterpillar to Butterfly   49

DEDICATION

I dedicate this book to my daughter, son, and
generations of family members.

I also dedicate this book to my loving friend,
Grace Vergis, who edited this book.

HEALING FROM PERSONAL TRAUMAS

INTRODUCTION

My name is Claudette Betty. I began my healing journey when I was forty-two years of age, after experiencing problems with my husband's behavior while under the influence of alcohol, a behavior that was all too familiar to me because my father was an alcoholic. I was concerned that my husband was becoming an alcoholic because he was displaying the very same behavior I had observed of my father while intoxicated.

I read self-healing books for two years prior to establishng my private counseling practice. Louise Hay's book "You Can Heal Your Life" became my bible for my own healing throughout the different seasons of my life. My counselor informed me that I needed to stop reading those books and apply what I had learned from her in my everyday life. She told me that I had developed academy award survival skills to function in my dysfunctional home, which consisted of my parents and four brothers who were bullies. I needed to identify my negative thoughts, irrational beliefs and suppressed emotions in order to develop the effective coping skills to change my behavior. Once this was accomplished, she told me that I would need to practice my new coping skills and let go of my survival skills. I was warned that this process may instill fear in me because I had become dependent on my survival skills. Whenever I attempted to use my new coping skills, anxiety would set in and I had severe panic attacks. I realized that I was dependent on my old coping skills because I trusted them to keep me safe. Eventually I began to trust the coping skills my counselor had taught me when I noticed that my life was changing for the better because of them. Whenever I felt helpless, hopeless and powerless, I listened to "I will survive" by Gloria Gaynor and " I am a woman" by Helen Reddy.

Throughout my healing journey, I became a Registered Nurse, B.S. Addiction Counselor, Certified Holistic Nurse, Reiki Master and Shaman Practitioner.

I was introduced to Adult Children of Alcoholic Group Therapy, Gestalt Therapy, Family Therapy and eventually Intensive Therapy, all of which helped me deal with the suicide deaths of my two brothers, and my father. While undergoing therapy, a repressed and traumatic episode of my mother when I was five years of age surfaced. I will be sharing all my traumatic experiences and recovery in my book.

Traumatic events affect the body, mind, emotions, and ultimately one's behavior. They are classified as witnessing or experiencing the sudden or violent death of a loved one or others you care about, as well as, serious physical injury, molestation, sexual, physical, mental, emotional abuse by family members, spouse or person in society. Mental effects of trauma include heightened awareness, dissociation from emotional pain, denial of the event happening, difficulty concentrating, poor attention span, memory problems, and nightmares. Emotional effects include fear, inability to feel safe, loss of trust in self and others, loss of self-esteem, shame, guilt, anger, feeling numb and overwhelmed. Physical effects include anxiety, depression, panic attacks, fatigue, elevated vital signs, and stomach distress. When these symptoms are not addressed by a medical doctor or a therapist and worsen after three months, post-traumatic stress disorder can become evident.

CHAPTER 1

Childhood Trauma

My parents, Napoleon and Jeanne (whom we called Mama and Papa), did not understand how their behavior affected their six children. They learnt their behavior from their parents. Although they are not with me now, I know they would be proud of my willingness to share the traumas I endured throughout my life. My goal is to not only educate, counsel, and share my healing process, but to also heal the next generation of family members.

When I was five years old, I was awakened by my mother's screams. My five brothers and myself ran down the stairs from our bedrooms to witness my father beating up our mother while he was under the influence of alcohol. My brothers pulled him off her, but he started hitting them. My oldest brother ran to a neighbor's house because we did not have a telephone and asked them to call the police. When the police arrived, my father was handcuffed and taken to jail. As he left, he threatened to hurt my mother for sending him to jail.

Fear for our lives motivated my mother to take us to the lake where we lived and tie a rope around herself and all her children with the intent of pushing us into the lake and drowning us all. Fortunately, my oldest brother, Roland, managed to get himself out of the rope and stopped her from fulfilling her plan. After this incident, we went back to our house and lived in fear of our father's return. When he returned from jail, he

1

told us that he was going back to Canada to live. We did not have any money while he was gone, therefore we survived by eating the food from my mother's garden, eating her chickens and eggs, and drinking Billy the goat's milk. After three months of being in Canada, our father returned to our home and everything seemed to go back to normal. The trauma we endured was never brought up again.

Unfortunately, I did not have any knowledge of the negative effects that this trauma would have on my mind, body, emotions, and behavior. Instinctively, I developed survival skills to cope with the trauma. Mentally, I dissociated myself from the incident by denying it ever happened. Emotionally, I repressed my feelings of fear and depression over the belief that my mother didn't love me or that I was not good enough to live. I took the role in my dysfunctional home of hero and lost child. I lost myself in the care of others and spent time in the woods sitting on a big rock overlooking a beautiful town to avoid being around my father and brothers. My belief in God was the moving force that kept me safe and sane. Physically I had anxiety which caused me to be hyperactive all the time. No matter how much I ate, I never gained weight. As a result of all of this, I ended up having gastric problems which required hospitalization.

When I was in the sixth grade, my teacher molested me. He would instruct me to move over and sat in my seat at my small desk. He would then start to run his hands up my leg until I pushed him out of the seat. My parents and Principal did not believe me when I told them what had happened. It took a classmate of mine to get pregnant by this teacher for them to realize that I was telling the truth. Upon investigation, it was discovered that he was fired from a school in Texas for the same behavior. This trauma caused me to not trust any of my male teachers. I did not want to attend public school after I graduated, therefore I informed my parents that I wanted to attend a catholic school where the nuns and priests would keep me safe. My father was very stingy with his money but agreed to pay for my high school education at a catholic school. I did feel safe in this school.

2

That same year, Carol, my best friend from first grade with whom I had a special sister-like relationship, moved to another town. I was devastated and missed her terribly. When Carol was in the seventh grade, my parents received a phone call from Carol's parents informing them that when Carol got off the school bus, she was hit by a car while crossing the street. She sustained several fractures and needed to be hospitalized. When my parents and I visited her in the hospital, I felt pain in the pit of my stomach when I saw her hooked up to all the machines. She remained in the hospital for three months. It would have helped me to have knowledge of the grief process at that time. The law in Connecticut that states "Do not pass a bus while the stop sign was out" was passed after my best friend's accident.

When I was twelve years old, I was swimming in the lake when I witnessed a girl who lived in one of the cottages on our street, go under water and not come up. Even though I was a good swimmer, I didn't have the lifesaving skills I needed to save her. I did go under water and kept pushing her up until someone came to her rescue. I never knew her name nor did I have the opportunity to speak with her because her family members took her home immediately. Ironically, in 2017, a nursing classmate of mine gave this girl (whose name is Betty) the first book I ever wrote titled "Creating a Wholesome Human Being". When she read it, she called me up to thank me for saving her life. She told me that she spent several years trying to locate the person who had rescued her from drowning. It made me feel good to finally get to know the individual I helped so many years ago. Prior to speaking with her, I had nightmares for years after that incident.

I never shared any of my childhood traumas with anyone until the age of 42 when I underwent therapy. During my adulthood, I worked on a children's behavioral health unit where schools would send children with behavioral problems that were beyond their control. Parents also sent their children to this unit when they were unable to control their child's behavior. I loved working with these children. When I asked them if they had a coping skill for anger, they would ask "What is that?". I would respond that anger is a strong emotional feeling. It can feel like anxiety, frustration, irritability, fear, rage, and hostility. Physically, you can feel knots in your stomach, your teeth and fist become clenched, and you have

3

a desire to hurt someone. The children often asked me what I did when I got angry. I responded that I would talk to my counselor about my anger. She suggested that I go to a safe environment and scream into a pillow or beat up my mattress with a foam bat to physically release the anger. These children told me that they would try those coping skills as well. When I asked them what they did when they became depressed, they would again ask "What is that?". I responded that it was a feeling of sadness, sorrow, lack of energy and motivation. They asked me what I did when I became sad. I responded that I would talk to my counselor, take a walk, ride my bicycle, do yoga, and watch comedies. I believe that parents and teachers should be educated on the different emotions we experience as human beings, explain them to children, teach them the appropriate coping skills and observe their use of those coping skills. It would also help parents to understand what codependency is and how it affects their children's behavior. Unfortunately, many of these children's parents would not pick them up when they were discharged. We would have to call DCF to pick them up and bring them home to their parents. All the above-mentioned behaviors could be resolved with family therapy.

CHAPTER 2

Teenage Trauma

While growing up, my parents always spoke French with myself and my five brothers. When we started grade school, we were unable to communicate in English. The Principal advised my parents to speak English to us for us to be able to continue attending school. I loved the learning process and always got good grades. I was constantly intrigued with the world, its objects and with people's behavior. My desire to discover my true authentic self has always been the driving force behind my actions. My brothers didn't like school and became the school bullies. The Principal often hit them with a leather belt in the school's hallway. They never screamed or cried because my father told them that they needed to be strong and never show emotion. I wanted to hide or leave the scene because I felt embarrassed, sad, and angry about their behavior in school. My father never supported my mother in disciplining them because he thought fighting showed that they were strong. They bullied other children in our neighborhood. The parents of those children called the police who frequently came to our home. I learned later when undergoing therapy that my father's physical and verbal abuse of my brothers activated their bullying behavior. It was their way of releasing anger and taking the focus off my father's behavior when he was intoxicated.

We lived in a home that overlooked a beautiful lake. We would skate in the winter, swim in the summer, and row our boat across the lake to get ice cream. We would also fish with a bamboo pole which held a worm with a safety pin attached to a string. My parents would have to come down to the lake to fetch us for our meals. We also lived close to a country club that had golfing in the summer and big hills on which we would sleigh ride and toboggan. Our outdoor games consisted of baseball, tag football, hide and seek, cowboys and Indians, hiking in the woods and walking on stilts. Those times brought us much happiness and made up for the bad times. I was mature for my age and loved being with young children, therefore I became the babysitter for most of the families who lived around our lake. We didn't have much money so the money I received from babysitting helped me become independent. To this day, I remain financially independent and will not ask anyone for money.

When I was sixteen years old, my mother who was forty-two years of age, gave birth to my baby brother on Thanksgiving Day. This was also my birthday. I had prayed for a sister to play with instead of always being surrounded by my brothers. I was angry at God and my mother for not giving me the sister I always wished for. This feeling caused me to avoid my younger brother's presence when he came home from the hospital with my mother. I ignored him until I noticed how difficult it was for my mother to raise him. At that time people believed that it was shameful to get pregnant at her age and were very vocal about it. I took on the role of mother and would ride around the neighborhood with Robert in a carriage thus taking the stigma off my mother.

The street which I lived on had cottages which people would rent for the summer. I became friendly with several girls my age. I met a girl by the name of Ann Marie Picard when I was twelve years old who still is my best friend to this day. My neighbor was Patricia Andrews. Even though she was four years older than I, we enjoyed playing together. She was an only child and gave me all the beautiful clothes she had outgrown. Her clothes made me feel important and accepted. My mother would not let me go out with her at night because I was too young. This angered me to the point the I would go to my room, stomp my feet, and slam my desk drawers open and shut. However, my behavior did not change my mom's mind. When I was sixteen years old, she allowed me to date and my brothers would check out the boys that I dated. I was naive and never believed that anyone would ever hurt me.

My brothers would always bully my friends and I when we swam in the lake. They would dunk our heads under the water and not let us up. I learned to count to one hundred under water to cope with their behavior. Roland and Jules, my two oldest brothers, joined the Air Force when they were eighteen years old to get away from our family environment. Although they bullied me at times, they protected me from harm and always made sure I was safe. I did miss them when they were gone. Donald, who was the third oldest brother, became a mechanic. He did not like school and would fix the things that were broken in the classroom while class was in session. When he was in the second grade, he was fixing the piano when his teacher grabbed him and wrapped a rope around him tying him to a chair. He managed to get out of the rope and walked home on the main road which was a half hour from school. My mother was so angry that she went to the school to talk to the Principal. The teacher was disciplined and later on we heard that she committed suicide. She was obviously depressed. This trauma affected my brother's mind, body, emotions and behavior throughout his life.

CHAPTER 3

Adult Trauma

I lived in the residential town of Wolcott, Connecticut and needed to take a bus to Sacred Heart High School which was in the city of Waterbury. I would attend mass every morning before going to school at Sacred Heart Church which was next to the school. I would talk to God and ask him to keep me safe and help me enjoy my high school experience. I lacked self-esteem; therefore, I did not mingle well with my classmates. I only hung out with the studious ones. I was on the honor roll which made my parents and I proud. Being on the honor roll elevated my self-esteem and gave me the confidence to socialize with other classmates. Eventually, I made several friends and started to date boys and attend parties which affected my grades. I didn't experience any trauma in high school. Because I had a good experience in a catholic high school, I decided to enter a three-year diploma catholic nursing school with a friend that I had met when I was twelve years old. Her family was the first family I met that had parents and family members who interacted in a healthy manner with one another. Even though I always had friends whose families were like mine, I began to understand that some families were different from mine. I enjoyed being in their presence. They made me feel comfortable.

I loved living in a Nurse's Dormitory and met lots of new friends. I felt a sense of freedom being away from home. We would have classes with the Sisters of Mercy who monitored us constantly for the first three months and then we worked in the hospital on different units. I loved applying what I had learnt on my patients. We entertained our patients and made them laugh as we gave them a bath in the morning, served their meals, cleaned off their trays and kept their rooms clean. We followed our priest every morning to deliver communion to our patients. When a doctor entered our unit, we stood up, got his patients' charts, followed him to visit every patient and catered to his every need. My favorite place to work was on the surgical unit because I was able to witness the daily healing of my patients. I couldn't heal my own family, but I was instrumental in healing my patients which made me feel good.

We needed to spend three months working with Tuberculosis and Psychiatric affiliations outside of our city. I didn't enjoy working in the Tuberculosis hospital because the patients were isolated in their rooms. We needed to wash our hands in a bacterial solution, wear a mask, gloves, and gown before entering each room. I liked physical contact with clients. My psychiatric affiliation was more exciting because I learned a lot about mental illness and all the different treatments they received. On some units we needed to be careful when interacting with patients because the manic ones could harm us. At that time, alcoholics were admitted to mental hospitals because of their behavior while under the influence of alcohol. When they became sober, they became a different person. It reminded me of my father's behavior whenever he drank. When he was sober, he was kind but when he was intoxicated, he was mean. When sober, the patient's demeanor was "Come Here" but when intoxicated, their demeanor was "Go Away". The mind always fascinated me, and, in my studies, I began to understand some of the behavior psychiatric patients exhibited. I also started to understand the behavior of my own family members. We had to read the patients biopsychosocial records and I noticed that most of them had been mentally, physically, and emotionally traumatized. Family members were not counseled while the patients were hospitalized. Thus, patients were discharged to the same family environment and often readmitted. Throughout the thirty years I worked with psychiatric, drug and alcoholic clients, I would ask my supervisors and doctors why family members were not considered a part of the patient's recovery. Nowadays, family therapy is widely recognized because all illnesses affect the family unit. The only time I noticed changes in a patient's behavior was when family members were involved in their healing process.

One morning, I received a phone call from one of my friends who told me that she was going to pick me up at the hospital to bring me home to visit with our friends. When we got to my home, I learned that my brother, Roland, had died in a car accident. He was twenty-one years old and had been in the Korean war where he was captured and imprisoned. My mother explained that he had been visiting his girlfriend in Main. He went to work with her brother and when they were driving back home, the weather became foggy. Her brother ran into the truck in front of them which was carrying steel pipes which went through Roland's head killing him and his girlfriend's brother instantly. I felt angry that he survived the Korean War only to be killed in a car accident. He drank heavily when he came back home from the war and never spoke about his experience in the war. He sedated his emotions with alcohol and eventually became an alcoholic. I wasn't informed that the National Guard would be giving him a 21-gun salute. When the guns went off, I collapsed to the ground and sobbed uncontrollably. He had been my protector and I would miss him, and the comedian role he took in our family. I asked my mother why she didn't cry nor express anger nor sadness at Roland's wake and funeral. She said that her parents taught her to never show her emotions in public, therefore she grieved in private. She was my role model for expressing emotions. When I went back to the psychiatric hospital, I dealt with Roland's death by drinking alcohol more than usual. The scary treatments that I witnessed in the care of my patients was another reason to drink in order to forget the emotional impact they had on me. I witnessed electric and insulin shock treatments that were supposed to change brain chemistry to relieve depression. Patients were hosed down with crisscross hot and cold water while others were put into a hot tub with only their heads exposed to help manic and anxiety patients relax. I believed these treatments were inhumane.

I was so glad to finally get back to my own hospital to work until I graduated in 1957. I worked on the medical/surgical unit for two years. Not only did we cater to our doctor's every need which I felt interfered

11

with our patient's needs, but we were under the constant supervision of the Nuns. It was very stressful. At the time, I weighed one hundred pounds and lost ten pounds due to all the stress, so I decided to go work at Waterbury Hospital which was in our city. The unit they assigned me to provided special care to patients who donated large amounts of money to the hospital. The patients had sterling silver coffee containers unlike the other units. The atmosphere was relaxed, and my supervisor was a compassionate nurse. I regained the ten pounds I had lost because I was no longer under stress. I felt happy when working and enjoyed caring for my patients without interruptions.

CHAPTER 4

Marital Years of Trauma

When I was eighteen years old, I met Jack at a roller-skating rink. He was with his friend, Vance, watching the skaters. Vance, whom I knew since grammar school, introduced me to Jack who was not only good looking but looked very handsome in his army uniform. Jack called to ask me out on a date which I accepted. We enjoyed each other's company and had a great time together. The longer we dated, the more I noticed his kindness, honesty, and desire to care for my wellbeing. When we introduced each other to our family members, we discovered that both he and his two brothers (who were born a year apart) and my mother and brother all shared the same birth date, March 8th. We had several birthday gatherings on that date. I enjoyed interacting with his four sisters especially since I never had a sister.

Jack was sent to Japan for two years while I was working and studying for my Nursing degree. We wrote to each other frequently while I continued to date other men. I dated a man whom I knew from childhood. He was our milkman's son. His name was Rodney. His family came often to visit us and to swim in our lake. When Rodney asked me to go steady, I hesitated because I feared hurting Jack's feelings. At the time, I liked both Jack and Rodney. It was emotionally painful for me to write Jack informing him of my relationship with Rodney. He wrote me a letter back expressing his anger because he believed we were going steady. However, I had never made that commitment to him. Recently, I began to evaluate why I made this decision and concluded that it was because Jack was away in Japan and Rodney was nearby and available. The feeling of love was not familiar to me. I never observed my parents show any affection like hugs or kisses to one another. However, I did witness my mother being mentally, emotionally, and physically abused.

After graduating from St Mary's Hospital School of Nursing in 1957, I broke off my relationship with Rodney when he began to tell me how to live my life. I became depressed over male relationships and decided to hang out with my girlfriends and my family members. Jack re-entered my life after returning home from the Army. He found out through my brother Roland that I had broken up with Rodney. He called me to ask me out on a date and we discussed the issue of my breaking off our relationship. We dated for a year, got engaged and decided to get married on January 17, 1959. We frequently socialized with three of my closest friends in nursing school and their husbands. We all drank alcohol at our gatherings, danced, laughed, and enjoyed life.

Jack and his father had a Fire Extinguisher business from which he made fifty-two dollars a week and I made fifty-four dollars a week working at Waterbury Hospital. I remember having an accordion envelope where I would put aside five dollars a week to pay for the furniture and appliances we bought for our apartment. We lived on his paycheck and put the money from my paycheck in the bank to buy a house.

In 1960, after one year of marriage, I became pregnant and continued working until I was six months pregnant, which was the rule at that time for pregnant nurses. Jack and his father bought a large building to house their business and opened a restaurant where his mother and sister worked. I was asked to work at the restaurant when I stopped working at the hospital. One day while I was working alone, a busload of children came into the restaurant and ordered all types of food. I became stressed trying to keep up with the multitude of orders and felt a strange movement in my stomach. My sister-in-law came to relieve me while I went to see my Obstetrician who informed me that my baby had flipped and would be born breach. I decided to focus on taking care of myself until the baby was born. When I went into labor, our baby was delivered stillborn. Two of my nurse friends were with me in the delivery room and became hysterical when Rita was born dead. After this incident occurred, only delivery room nurses were allowed in the delivery room. When I awoke and heard about my baby's death, I went into both shock and denial. Because I hadn't learnt how to process grief, I remained in denial for a long time. Feeling ill at the time of Rita's burial, I was not able to attend the ceremony. My family took care of all the arrangements and had her buried next to my brother, Roland, at the cemetery. Jack and I never spoke of her death again. Subconsciously, I believe we both felt guilty and blamed ourselves for her death when she was born with a hole in her heart, cleft palate, and hair lip. It wasn't until three years later that I grieved her death while taking a shower in our new home. I burst out crying hysterically for a half an hour calling out her name. Jack thought I was having a nervous breakdown. Releasing my grief made me feel better and helped me get on with my life.

I finally returned to work to do private duty nursing. I cared for one client eight hours a day giving me the opportunity to focus on his/her total care without interruption from outside sources. Several of my patients asked me to care for them in their homes after being discharged from the hospital. This was a new challenge for me because I didn't have any of the resources that were available to me while working in a hospital. I felt empowered with this new nursing responsibility. While caring for one of my patients in her home on New Year's Day, she vomited blood and needed to be hospitalized. I had plans with Jack for New Year's Eve, but no nurses were available to do private duty at the hospital, therefore I remained until a nurse became available. The family was very grateful and gave me a $500.00 bonus. I bought a dishwasher with that money. The hospital registry called me to do private duty nursing with a patient who was in the intensive care unit for two weeks and was discharged to our medical unit. I discovered that he was an alcoholic with alcohol related illnesses. He had an intravenous saline drip running, a gastric tube inserted for liquid feedings and a catheter for urinary drainage. His doctor left an order to give Spirits of Fermenti (medical terminology for whisky) through his gastric tube. I informed the doctor that the client was an alcoholic who had been detoxed in Intensive Care. Most of our doctors weren't educated in drug and alcohol addiction, therefore he told me to do as he ordered, or he would tell my supervisor to take me off the case. After this incident, I noticed that several of my patients were addicted to alcohol and pain pills. Doctors would order pain pills and injections for long periods of time. Before it became illegal, we gave intramuscular normal saline as a placebo effect when patients frequently requested pain medication. The placebo inevitably relieved their pain because their mind and body had become addicted to pain medication. Because of this awareness, I decided to go back to college to learn about addiction and eventually work in a Drug and Alcohol Rehabilitation Center.

I had to put this plan on hold when I became pregnant again in 1962. I attended mass every day for nine months to pray for a healthy baby. We were ecstatic when Karen was born healthy. We enjoyed having her in our lives and we played with her every day. Not long after her birth, my father's drinking problem escalated, and he aggressively hit my mother on several occasions. My brothers, Jack and I decided to move her and my brother Robert, who was fifteen at that time, out of their home to live with us in our apartment. This was when we decided it was time to build our new home.

My brother-in-law built our home in the country where I lived as a child. Our house had three large rooms on the first floor and three bedrooms on the second floor. We converted our basement into a social room with a bar. My mother and Robert moved into our new home with us. Jack and my mother got along well which made her living with us easier. In 1964, when Karen was one-and-a-half years old, I became pregnant again, and gave birth to Kevin who was also a healthy baby, He brought such joy to our lives. My mother would babysit for us when we attended social events and went on vacations. She helped raise our children resulting in Kevin and Karen being very close to her. Their friends would ask, "How come you have two mothers?". My mother tried to get a divorce from my father, but the judge told her that she managed to tolerate his behavior for twenty-five years and saw no reason why she couldn't remain in the marriage. She was furious that the judge condoned my father's abusive behavior. My father made several attempts to have her move back home, but she always refused.

When Robert began to get into trouble in our neighborhood, my mother decided to get an apartment to alleviate our involvement.

In 1972, at the age of thirty-four, my brother Donald was diagnosed with acute glomerulonephritis which is an inflammation of the tiny filters to the kidney called glomeruli. His doctor told him that his condition stemmed from a strep throat infection for which he neglected to receive medical treatment. The treatment for his condition consisted of antibiotics, diuretics, and dialysis. His insurance wouldn't pay for his treatments because dialysis was new and expensive at that time. He worked as a mechanic and couldn't pay for dialysis. Family members were unable to help him pay for treatments because his doctor told us that his condition was chronic and dialysis would need to take place at a hospital two hours away three days a week for as long as he lived. His wife would call me whenever his body would fill up with toxic fluid causing him shortness of breath and severe anxiety. I would call an ambulance to transport him to the hospital where he received oxygen and diuretics. He would visit me at my home when he felt well, sit in a chair and stare at me. I felt helpless, hopeless, and powerless because I couldn't help him get well. At the time, I couldn't identify depression but felt sad most days. One day while he was visiting, I wanted to cry and scream but managed to suppress my emotions. My body became numb and I couldn't move off the couch. I asked Donald to call Jack who took me to the emergency room. After answering a lot of questions, my doctor told me I had experienced hysterocatalepsy which is caused by depression, anxiety, and suppression of emotions. He gave me a shot of Ativan to subside my symptoms. After continuing to help Donald with his health condition, I began to hemorrhage vaginally. My Obstetrician told me that I needed to have a dilatation and curettage which is a surgical procedure to scrape the uterine lining to discover the source of bleeding. I felt well for a while, but eventually continued to hemorrhage. My blood hemoglobin went down to 8.2 which made my doctor decide to perform a hysterectomy on me at the age of thirty-six. When I returned home from the hospital, my mother helped me with my recovery.

The next morning when my mother and husband went to work, I received a phone call from my Uncle in Canada asking me what time

Donald's funeral was taking place. I was speechless and told him that I would call him back. When I called Jack to ask when Donald had died and what had happened to him, he told me that Donald had committed suicide by ingesting poison. He was unable to live with his condition any longer. My mother and Jack were concerned about my recovery; Thus why they didn't tell me about Donald's death. Again, I felt guilty and shameful for not being able to help him in his despair. My lack of strength prevented me from attending his funeral. I felt depressed and angry over his death and had a long difficult recovery from my hysterectomy. My mother and Jack became concerned over my lack of energy and willingness to resume my normal activities. Together they decided for all of us to take a vacation to visit my brother Jules and his family in Texas. We bought our children cowboy and cowgirl outfits with boots and gun holsters. Karen was seven years old and Kevin was five years old at the time. After two weeks, my mother flew home while we continued our trip to Arizona. The dry air and beautiful scenery lifted my spirits making me feel alive again. We went to Grand Canyon National Park which had rocks and mountains with orange and red colors flowing through them. Jack, Karen and I were in awe of the beautiful scenery but when Karen asked Kevin "Why are you looking for Indians to shoot and not enjoying the scenery?", he replied "I only see rocks". We had to remember that he was only five years old. After visiting Utah and Colorado which we loved, we decided to return home.

Jack and his father sold the building that housed their business and built an even bigger building for the Fire Extinguisher business. They eventually also built apartment buildings. The business became financially successful allowing us to travel across country with our children as well as invest in an inground pool. We had Karen and Kevin take swimming lessons and did not allow any children who couldn't swim to enter the pool area. All our friends, family members and neighbors always talked about the many picnics we hosted at our home. Raising our children, attending their many activities, and traveling with them were enjoyable years. Karen and Kevin had fun with their friends. They ice skated, swam in our pool and the lake where I used to live, skied, bicycled, and went sleigh riding.

Showing up daily as a happy, cheerful, and energetic person kept my children, friends, and family from knowing how all my past traumas had negatively impacted me mentally, physically, and emotionally. My definition of ego is presenting oneself to the outside world as you would like them to know you, while self-esteem is presenting yourself as your true authentic self which I wasn't willing to do until now, as I'm writing this book.

In 1974, I received a phone call from my mother telling me that my father had committed suicide by hanging himself at home. A neighbor hadn't seen him in a few days and called my brother Raymond who found our father hanging from a rope in our childhood home. Once again, I went into shock feeling shame and guilt for not being able to help my father stop drinking. I had a love-hate relationship with my father. His behavior always reminded me of the movie Dr. Jekyll and Mr. Hyde. When he was sober, he was Dr. Jekyll and when he was intoxicated, he was Mr. Hyde. We had a family-only ceremony and never discussed his death after the ceremony. Raymond bought the house from my mother and moved his wife and three sons into that house. While remodeling the house, he found thousands of dollars hidden behind a cabinet within the kitchen wall and in areas of the garage. He gave some of the money to my mother and kept the rest. Finding my father hanging from a rope affected his mind and emotions causing him extreme agony. He left his family to go to Arizona, Las Vegas, and Texas where he squandered the money on native jewelry, drinking and gambling. He neglected to provide money for his family, therefore we helped them survive the best we could. It was five years before we saw Raymond again. We were all angry at my father for hiding money and denying our needs.

Jack began to stop at bars after work and would come home late for dinner. We had several arguments about this new behavior, but he continued to go to bars. After some time, he would stop coming home altogether for dinner. And when he did come home, he was always intoxicated. I became concerned because his behavior reminded me of my father. I did not want our children to witness our arguments, so I repressed my emotions and eventually had panic attacks and stomach issues which caused me to be hospitalized. My doctor diagnosed me with severe anxiety related to stress and suggested that we seek counseling. Jack was resistant to seeing a counselor because he didn't believe he had a drinking problem. I told him that his behavior when he drank caused me to become anxious and depressed. He finally agreed to see a counselor with me. Yolanda, our counselor, advised me to partake in the Adult Children of Alcoholic group sessions while she advised Jack to attend Twelve Step meetings. Yolanda was the facilitator of our ACOA group of six people. She informed us that we all grew up in dysfunctional homes where the behavior of a family member, while under the influence of alcohol, controlled other family members via their negative words, irrational beliefs, and inappropriate behavior. The result: a confused child who is seeking love, kindness, and acceptance. In a private session, Yolanda asked me what behaviors helped me cope with my family dynamics. I was unable to process and evaluate her question at that time. After pondering for a while what we had discussed, I was able to tell her in my next session that I created a fantasy world by frequently reading a big book of fairy tales to avoid living in the reality of my family environment. I also went into the woods to sit on a big rock and enjoy the serenity of nature. Dissociating from my body whenever I felt emotional pain was another survival technique I used. She gave me a list of negative words and irrational beliefs that ACOA children hear and believe to be true. We needed to change these words and beliefs to positive ones. Understanding how my father's behavior, while under the influence of alcohol, affected my life helped me realize that I wasn't to blame for his behavior. It gave me hope for the future. I learned that alcoholism is a chronic disorder marked by excessive and compulsive drinking of alcohol leading to psychological and physical dependency on alcohol. Regardless of this knowledge, I still couldn't comprehend his choice to continue drinking when we had a good life. I told him that there wasn't any reason to abuse alcohol. Yolanda explained to me that the disease of alcoholism is a baffling, cunning and powerful one which renders family members powerless to help drug and alcoholic people stop drinking and using drugs.

I shared my newfound knowledge with Jack who continued to deny his drinking was a problem and refused to attend AA meetings. I decided to go to college like I planned in 1962 before I learned that I was pregnant. I wanted to learn more about drug and alcohol addiction. Our community college offered an Associate Degree in Drug and Alcohol Counseling. After attending two years of school, I was required to spend another two years taking counseling courses followed by an internship which I did at the hospital from which I graduated. I got a job as a Staff Detox Nurse at Gaylord Hospital. I took care of all my patients' needs when I worked in hospitals, therefore it was an adjustment to allow my patients to be responsible for their own behavior and needs while in treatment I attended AA meetings with my patients and heard their stories about the use of alcohol and drugs and how it affected their lives. I learned that Bill Wilson founded Alcoholic Anonymous in 1935. He was an alcoholic who ruined a promising career on Wall Street by his inability to stop drinking. After Bill was hospitalized four times due to his compulsive use of alcohol, he cried out while lying in bed depressed and despairing "I'll do anything! Anything at all! If there be a God, let Him show himself!". He then had the sensation of a bright light, a feeling of ecstasy and new serenity. (Wikipedia "History of Alcoholic Anonymous") Believing that two sober people could help keep each other sober caused him to go on a crusade to find another alcoholic with whom he could remain sober. He found Bob Smith, a medical and surgical doctor who was also an alcoholic. His medical practice was in jeopardy due to his behavior while under the influence of alcohol. They stayed sober together by surrendering to a power greater than themselves, attending AA meetings with other alcoholics every day and obtaining a sponsor to help work the twelve steps of the AA program. After reading the 12 steps of AA, I believed they would work for every human being as a way of life. I shared this new knowledge with Jack, but he was not interested.

My youngest brother Robert, whom I helped raise, started to use drugs and alcohol, and needed to be admitted three times to rehabilitation centers. My mother was devastated over the behavior of her sons. I tried to educate her about the disease of drug and alcoholism, but she believed it was a mark of weakness. While eating dinner one evening, my brother Raymond knocked on our door. He was intoxicated and very distressed. He informed us that Robert was arrested for the possession of drugs and hung himself in jail. To block out this news, I became numb and still do not remember attending Robert's funeral. One day when my mother and

21

I were visiting our family's cemetery plot, she asked me to weed around Robert's burial site. I told her that I didn't know where it was. Her response was "You buried his ashes over your brother Donald". This was when we both realized how damaged I really was due to the numerous deaths in our family. I knew I needed to enter therapy again to not only deal with these deaths, but also to address my anxiety and depression.

I used to take my mother to Rhode Island for weekend vacations where we enjoyed one another's company and she would share her childhood memories with me. On one of those weekends, I was swept ashore by a big wave. Upon standing up, I fractured three bones in my left ankle. The experience was traumatic and so was my hospital stay. Three years later, I had the hardware removed to prevent me from having ankle arthritis in the future. Recently when the weather got cold, I experienced inflammation in my left ankle causing it to swell up and be very painful. I tried to nurse my ankle with medical and alternative treatments, but nothing seemed to work. One night while focusing on my ankle, I became overwhelmed with emotional pain causing me to cry uncontrollably. After ten minutes of crying, the pain in my ankle subsided and the swelling went down. This experience helped me to understand cellular memory. I subconsciously repressed the emotions from that incident into my cellular memory. Cellular memory is held in our cells, tissues, and muscles without our knowledge. Releasing my emotions in turn released the residual physical pain.

CHAPTER 5

Healing Years

Jack and I went to a friend's funeral and then afterwards we went for a drink to a bar we often frequented. We had discovered that alcohol was the medicine that helped deal with grief. When I wanted to go home, Jack said that he was not ready to leave. In the past, we had gotten into the habit of drinking with our friends until the bars closed. My quest to heal myself prevented me from following this pattern of behavior anymore. I left the bar and walked home vowing to myself that I would never drink with him again. The thought of us becoming alcoholics put fear into my heart. I didn't want my children to live with two alcoholic parents as I had witnessed with several of our friends. After that episode, Jack became angry when I refused to drink with him at social events. He began to drink more, and his behavior caused me much mental and emotional distress. I made an appointment with Yolanda, my therapist, to discuss the idea of me getting a divorce. She suggested that we get family therapy with a male therapist she recommended. Jack was resistant but when Karen and Kevin encouraged their father to attend, he joined us. We had individual and family sessions with Ron, our family therapist, for three months. Our children watched us blame one another for our issues. Ron helped us understand that we both brought baggage into the relationship and that it was our responsibility to change our behavior to meet one another's needs. He also made Karen and Kevin aware of their predisposition to alcohol and drug addiction. We both had ancestors who had the disease of alcoholism. Our children were in their twenties at the time and worked with their father at the Waterbury Fire Extinguisher business. Even though I knew that our children went to parties with their friends that involved alcohol, I wasn't aware of any problems with them at the time. Jack stopped drinking for two months after family therapy to prove to himself that he wasn't an alcoholic. He eventually went back to drinking.

In 1989, I needed to go back to therapy. Yolanda suggested that I attend Gestalt Therapy. She explained that she would facilitate a group within an insulated room to allow free expression of emotions where the noise could not be heard outside of that room. Because I always embraced the advice of my therapist, I immediately started Gestalt Group Therapy with three females and three male clients. It frightened me when I listened to other clients scream and cry. I never gave myself permission to express my anger or sadness as it made me feel uncomfortable and embarrassed me. We never expressed emotions in our home while growing up because the message I got from my parents was "be strong and never show your emotions". After being in therapy for one month, I gathered up enough courage to scream and cry openly. While I was doing so, a volcano of emotions erupted causing me to cry uncontrollably. I felt a sense of relief from all the grief I had repressed over the years from my trauma experiences. In my next session, Yolanda asked me to sit in front of a mirror and say out loud, "It's time for you, Claudette". While saying this, I began to cry from the core of my being for fifteen minutes until I became utterly exhausted. We needed to process our feelings alone without interference from other members of the group. I realized that I always put the needs of others before my own needs from observing my mother behave in the very same manner. I began to truly understand that everything I had heard and observed during my childhood had a great impact on my life. We had to stand in front of the group and recite affirmations to elevate our self-esteem. An affirmation is a mental or verbal declaration to yourself and to the universe about what you need or desire out of life. For example, "I am an intelligent, competent, powerful and creative woman", "I love myself" and "I approve of myself". When they are repeated daily, they get impressed on the subconscious mind and eventually manifest into reality. After two months of attending Gestalt Therapy, I needed to take a break because my emotions were exhausted. Since I felt empowered after attending Gestalt Therapy in 1983, I encouraged both of my children to attend college out of state to get away from our dysfunctional home environment. Karen attended Northeastern College in Boston and Kevin attended Pepperdine University in California. They enjoyed being away, made several friends and did well at school. My goal was to make enough money to go to Florida and stay with my sister-in-law to find out if I would like to move there permanently after I got divorced.

I worked as staff detox nurse then as a head nurse at Gaylord Hospital from 1987 to 1991. My supervisor had asked me to motivate and persuade my staff nurses to get the Detox Certification that I had obtained by rewarding them with an additional dollar an hour wage increase. After two of my nurses had obtained their certification, they informed me that they did not get the extra dollar an hour increase in their paycheck. I mentioned this to my supervisor, and she denied ever telling me of this offer. I felt humiliated because she had made me look like a liar to my nurses. I remembered explicitly her stating this offer at a nurses' meeting where our secretary took notes. I asked her for the notes, made a copy of my supervisor's statement and sent it up to her supervisor. Before I made this move, I obtained another job as detox nurse at Blueridge Alcohol and Drug Rehabilitation Center in Bloomfield. My supervisor was surprised when I handed in my resignation. I was fully transparent with her and told her what I had done to ensure that my nurses get paid the dollar raise they deserved. When I left, those nurses thanked me for intervening on their behalf.

I worked at Blueridge Center from 1991 to 1995 as staff detox nurse. I was asked not only to be the nurse coordinator putting me in charge of the nursing staff, but I was also asked to resolve the dispute between the nursing and counseling staff. I had a meeting with both teams and discovered that the counseling staff worked sixty hours and were paid for forty hours. They were not being paid for comp time because of their inability to get the time off. They were angry at the nursing staff for getting full pay for forty hours. Our rehabilitation center was facilitated by a nearby hospital where my supervisor worked. I asked to have a meeting with her to resolve this issue. She managed to get the counselors their comp time. We all worked together as a harmonious unit afterwards. I enjoyed my new position even though I had to drive one hour to and from work daily in heavy traffic. I developed physiology lectures by showing a large picture of the human body with all the organs in color explaining how drugs and alcohol cause illnesses to those organs. Our clients were very receptive to visual information and asked several questions. Developing a pamphlet explaining the detox process and articles about drug and alcohol dependency helped patients to understand their addiction. The most effective information I delivered was the process of alcohol and drug addiction.

Alcohol and drug addiction is a disease with biological, neurological, genetic, and environmental source of origin. In the beginning stage of alcohol and drug use, people experiment with either one or both to discover how it effects the body and mind. A feeling of euphoria, tranquility and heightening of energy may prevail. Release from mental, emotional, and physical distress may also be experienced. If the person enjoys the feelings experienced during the experimental stage, there is a strong possibility that they will move into the abuse stage. Frequent misuse of alcohol and drugs to obtain the same feelings as in the experimental stage can create physical and mental dependency. Physical tolerance of larger doses occurs, and the mind craves alcohol and drugs to feel good. Whenever these substances are withheld from the system, physical and mental distress is experienced. Continued use of higher doses leads to the addictive stage. In the addictive stage, a pattern of compulsive use marked by a loss of control over the ability to regulate use or abstain is experienced. The addict begins to live an addictive lifestyle with others that use and encounters legal problems, loss of jobs, finances, family and friends and healthy social activities. Temporary or permanent mental disorders can result from the effect of chronic alcohol and drug poisoning to the brain. Physical tolerance excels and physical withdrawal symptoms are experienced when drugs and alcohol are withheld. The withdrawal symptoms from alcohol are elevated vital signs, anxiety, agitation, body tremors, nausea, and vomiting. The person requires detox with a drug having similar properties within a safe environment to avoid having a seizure. The withdrawal symptoms from opiate drugs are elevated vital signs, muscle aches and pain, anxiety, agitation, nausea, and vomiting. When detox is completed, a thirty-day rehabilitation program is recommended along with participation in the twelve-step program to receive education on relapse prevention and learn the proper coping skills to remain clean and sober. If a client relapses after this program, a sixty to ninety-day long term treatment program is recommended. Identifying irresponsible and self-defeating behavior and making healthy changes is vital. What one thinks and believes trigger emotions which activate behavior. Whenever I feel blocked, I ask myself "What do I want?", "What am I doing to get what I want?", "Is it working?", "If not, what can I do different?". This is a simple formula that works for me.

While writing my nursing notes on the detox unit, I felt a sudden surge of energy go through me, vibrating my body. I thought I was having a seizure. When it stopped, I looked up to find George, a counselor on our unit standing over me with a smile on his face. I was very confused and asked him if I could see him in private. I went to his office and shared what I had experienced. He smiled again and told me that he was a Shaman, and the energy of a Shaman recognizes the energy of another Shaman. He told me that the energy experience I felt was the connection of two Shamans who are in close proximity. I told him I didn't know what a Shaman was. He informed me that he ran a Shaman group every week and asked if I would be interested in joining to elevate my consciousness of Shamanism. I thought the whole situation was intriguing and agreed to join the group. I loved the Shamanic Journeys, Soul Retrievals, Vision Quest, and group counseling that we did, along with the new relationships I developed. We did Fire Ceremonies in the home of our group members who had a fireplace. I loved doing fire ceremonies. We stacked single pieces of kindling wood in tepee formation within the fireplace, balled up colored newspaper, put oil over the paper and lit it. Flowers were placed around the fireplace. The purpose of a fire ceremony is to place something you want to release into the fire in order to bring forth something that you desire. I placed a picture in which Jack, Karen and Kevin and I looked depressed into the fire so that it could bring forth for us a happier family life. Another way we released, was to give another group member something we were attached to that didn't serve a purpose in our life anymore. I was attached to a pearl ring Jack gave me but gave it to another girl to release my financial attachment to him. I loved participating in Shaman rituals but never had the desire to become a Shaman. After two years, our group ended resulting in George and I working together at a new level of consciousness.

Once I had saved enough money to get a divorce, I made plans to visit my sister-in-law in West Palm Beach, Florida. I obtained a lawyer, discussed my travel plans with Karen and Kevin, and finalized the itinerary with my friend Joan Lo Russo who joined me on my trip to Florida. While driving to Florida, Joan mentioned that she felt like she had the flu with a temperature, headache, muscle aches and pain. We belonged to an Edgar Casey study group and decided to stop in Virginia Beach to visit the Edgar Casey Foundation. She received a colonic irrigation to rid her of toxins and I got a massage to reduce my stress. We got a room right on the beach and slept twenty-four hours straight before we awakened. We could not believe that we had slept through the day. Joan felt much better and I felt more energetic. We had read "The Secrets of the Universe" about Walter Russel's life and his accomplishments with just a ninth-grade education so we decided to visit his school of energy in Virginia. When we stopped at the school of energy, we saw his sculptures, paintings, and the books he wrote. This man learned how to tap into universal consciousness. Throughout our friendship, Joan and I were always fascinated with the activities of the mind and universal energy. It took us a week to get to my sister-in-law's home where she lived with her sister and brother-in-law. Joan's husband flew down to spend time with her while I obtained a nurse's job with a woman residing in West Palm Beach. She had a female servant who attended to our meals while I delivered her medications and applied a back brace before taking her for a walk. Even though she was a pleasant woman and my tasks were minimal, I felt the need to be by myself at the beach to heal my body, mind, and emotions. Joan flew back home with her husband while I remained two more months swimming in the ocean, lying on the beach, praying, meditating, and cooking meals in the evening for the people I was rooming with. Kevin called me to say that his father was willing to have another family therapy session with Ron if I would come home. Jack seemed happy to see me and I was excited about the possibility of having Ron explain how beneficial it would be for him to enter a detox rehabilitation center. During our session with Ron, he asked me what I needed from Jack. I told him that I needed him to stop drinking. Jack asked Ron what was expected of him if he went to detox and rehabilitation. Ron explained everything to him but when he heard that he would not have a television in his room, he declined to go. Ron asked Jack what he needed from me and he said he that he needed me to get off his back about his drinking habit. After hearing this, I became very angry and told Jack I would do more than just get off his back, "I would get out of his life!". I finally had to admit to myself that I was powerless over his unwillingness to believe that his abuse of alcohol was problematic to our relationship. That is the moment I became estranged from Jack and started to move forward with my divorce plans. As I was doing everything in my power to make changes in my life, Jack informed me that he would pay for Karen to go to Europe with me if I would pay my own way. He knew I had saved enough money to live on my own. While this offer would use up most of my money, my desire to go to Europe was strong and I didn't want Karen to miss out on this opportunity. We made plans to visit Rome, Florence, Venice, France, Switzerland, and England. We both love history and found every place we visited interesting and educational. Karen studied the Renaissance period in school, therefore she helped me understand everything I saw in Rome. It was a very educational and exciting vacation. It gave Karen and I the opportunity to have quality time together.

After returning home from Europe, I made an appointment with Yolanda to tell her all about our trip and to fill her in on my future plans. I still wanted to move forward with my divorce but would have to save up more money to do so. When I was doing my counseling internship, a recruiter from the University of Connecticut came to our class and offered me thirty-six credits towards my Nursing Degree to attend UConn. At the time, I was not interested but I wanted to get a degree in counseling which was being offered at this college. My goal was to be well-rounded in knowledge and wisdom. I took one course a semester and graduated in 1996. In my creative writing class, my teacher asked us to get together with two other classmates to develop a creative project for class. I chose two female classmates at random and met with them at my home every week. We created a Utopia Planet in which we visualized ourselves as rabbits who lived on this planet which was full of beautiful trees, flowers, vegetables, fruits, and flowing rivers. All the rabbits living there were having fun, never yelled at one another, and exhibited compassion and love for each another. When we shared the project with our classmates, we held the rabbit puppets up toward the planet while describing what the rabbits discovered on their planet. They felt serenity and bliss. We felt good about our creative project, but our classmates and teacher were unable to understand the message. Our teacher told us to analyze the story to help her understand it. We got together to figure out a way to explain the message in our story. In doing so, we discovered that the three of us had an alcoholic parent. We shared our stories about living in a dysfunctional home with an alcoholic parent. That was when we really knew the message of our story. Subconsciously, we all wanted to create a world free of crises, arguments, and verbal abuse. The world we created was the world we wanted to live in. We shared this discovery with our teacher who gave us an "A" on our project. We were elated with our grade.

While attending classes, working, and trying to have a social life, I was experiencing anxiety issues. My stress management skills were not effective. I called Yolanda who informed me of a weekend workshop she was facilitating entitled "Healing Your Inner Child". She said that I had done a good job of healing and strengthening the adult within me, but I still needed to heal my inner-child. We had twelve people in our group. As I explored my childhood memories, Yolanda would not allow me to dissociate or numb my emotions. I felt like vomiting and had a strong desire to hide or leave the group. She kept me focused on my revelations and urged me to release my painful memories. As I did so, the memory of my mother's attempt to drown us surfaced. I shared my memory of this traumatic event while I cried and yelled out in anger. Yolanda explained to me and the other group members that my mother not only feared for her life and that of her children, but that she must have been so depressed at the time for her to attempt what she did. Depression can occur when a person is physically, mentally, and emotionally abused producing feelings of hopelessness, helplessness, and powerlessness. The workshop helped me understand why I always struggled with anxiety and fear. I felt some relief from my emotions but was exhausted and wanted to go to bed.

I called my mother daily to check on her wellness. She had glaucoma which affected her vision and interfered with her ability to read and watch television. Because there weren't any eye doctors in Connecticut who did laser treatments at the time of her diagnoses, I needed to bring her to Boston for treatments. The treatments kept her eyes from getting worse, but her vision never improved. My mother was my best friend and we had a great relationship. After finishing the workshop, I understood why I was always seeking her approval even when she repeatedly told me she was proud of my accomplishments. I idolized her. I saw her as a very strong person who had the ability to suppress her emotions. Over time however, not expressing one's emotions can cause one medical issues which is what happened to my mom. Taking care of and being generous with others was the model she lived by. She walked daily and spent lots of her time with her family and grandchildren. She was a beautiful and loving human being.

After returning home from the workshop, I went to my mother's apartment to visit her. When she didn't answer the door, I used my key to get in. When I didn't see her in any of the main rooms, I went into the bathroom to find her dead under water in her bathtub. I was hysterical. I called my children who weren't available because they were at a concert. I called my best friend, Ann Marie, who couldn't enter the apartment building without a pass, therefore she called Jack for help. The shock and circumstances of her death caused me to totally lose it. Jack helped me calm down enough to call the funeral home where my mother had made the arrangements to have her body cremated. The next person I called was Yolanda who told me to come to her office immediately after my mother's body was taken to the funeral home. Yolanda held me in her arms allowing me to cry for thirty minutes without interruption which helped me release the knife piercing pain I felt. I will always be grateful to her for her compassion and counseling. My brother Jules was flying in the next morning to celebrate my birthday which he did every year. He helped me make the funeral arrangements and have a family gathering afterwards. The funeral director told us that our mother had died of a heart attack. For a long time, I would still pick up the phone out of habit to call her and realize that she wasn't alive. Although my mom tried very hard to make up for our dysfunctional childhood, the memory of our father's behavior and the attempted drowning incident was trapped in our cellular memory, keeping us from making healthy life choices.

I miss my mom to this day and wish I could have made her life happier.

I had difficulty recovering from my mother's death and needed to have a counseling session with Yolanda. She asked me to attend a grief workshop in Antigua with six prestigious therapists from around the country. These therapists got together every year to work on their own issues. I was honored to participate and thought it was a great opportunity to do further grief work. My insurance paid for the one-week workshop with the diagnoses of "Adjustment Disorder". Most adult children of alcoholics have the diagnoses of "Adjustment Disorder" because they need to adjust to the reality of the real world. We had learned to use survival skills to adjust to life events. Our group consisted of twelve clients and six therapists besides Yolanda who facilitated the group. We spent four hours expressing our emotional pain and allowed the attending therapist to help us release the memories that caused the pain. I felt safe having the therapist hold me while allowing me to talk about the traumatic deaths of my family members. While I was sharing my story, I began to have a panic attack. I screamed and cried to release my anger and grief over the suicidal deaths and other deaths of my family members. The second four hours of the day were spent on a boat, swimming, fishing, and having fun. We needed to relax after exhausting our emotions. Massage therapy always made me feel good and balanced my body, therefore I had a massage on the beach by a native woman with the name of Claudette. She was the first black woman I ever met with my name. We spent five days going through therapy and playing afterwards. My creator put Yolanda into my life to help me heal my wounds, as well as placed other healers along my path to wellness.

Joan Lo Russo, my traveling companion suggested we take a trip to Arizona to relieve my stress. We had been on a spiritual journey together for several years and wanted to visit Sedona which is an energy vortex that has special spots where energy is more intense. We were both interested in spiritual energy, meditation, yoga, metaphysics, and new age music and studies. All this knowledge and practice kept transforming our lives. We stayed in a hotel in Phoenix and visited a Native American Indian Museum where we learned about Indian culture, arts, and crafts. We were fascinated with everything we heard and observed. The next day we rented a car and went to Sedona. We saw the Chapel of the Holy Cross which rises seventy feet out of a one thousand foot red-rock cliff. The cross was the most prominent feature. We also saw the cathedral and bell-rock. All these sights lifted our mood and we could feel the energy of the vortex fill our body and mind. We meditated while sitting on the rocks and hiked to view the wonderful scenery. The longer we stayed in Sedona, the more peaceful and serene we felt. The shops were full of beautiful handmade jewelry, pottery, and drums. I bought some jewelry and pottery, and Joan bought a Zulla drum made of buckskin. As we drove back to our hotel, we discussed our wonderful adventure. The next day we drove to Tucson where we visited the International Wildlife Museum. It had 400 lifelike taxidermist animals from all over the world. I was excited to view and get educated on these huge animals that stood behind glass. I always feared snakes but viewing them up close without the fear of being harmed allowed me to enjoy the moment and read all about them. The next building we visited was Biosphere 2 which is an earth systems science research facility located in Oracle, Arizona. Its mission is to service a center for research, outreach, teaching and lifelong learning about earth, its living systems, and its place in the universe. Eight people were selected to live in this glass enclosure for two years to prove that humans could sustain life by producing their own food and recycling waste and water while the rest of their time would be spent conducting ecological research. We were intrigued by the whole concept. After we visited the Old Tucson movie studio and took some pictures of us in western outfits, we decided to venture back to our hotel to get a good night's sleep before leaving in the morning.

After returning home from Arizona, I acknowledged that I had done everything in my power to keep my 36 years of marriage intact giving me the peace of mind I needed to move forward to finalize my divorce. Although it was emotionally painful knowing that our children's life would be impacted by the divorce, the fear of being financially independent and self-reliant had subsided with all the therapy I underwent.

CLAUDETTE BETTY

CHAPTER 6

New Beginnings

After our divorce was final, I continued to live in our home in Wolcott, while Jack lived in one of our apartments in Waterbury. I realized at the time that I couldn't maintain the house while working five days a week. So, Karen and Kevin helped me move out of our home and into one of our apartments, while Jack moved back into our house in Wolcott. My goal was to earn enough money to buy a condo in Avon, Connecticut which was closer to my workplace. Within a year, I had saved enough money to buy that condo in Avon. It was in a wooded area with lots of trees. The condos were freestanding and built like a tepee with glass windows in every room. Light radiated into all the rooms of my condo making me feel free, happy, and hopeful. I was so looking forward to living a blissful life.

Avon had alternative healing centers in the area which excited me. My creator always directed me to places where I could heal and grow in consciousness. I completed Reiki 1 with a nurse in Waterbury and found a woman in Avon with whom I could do Reiki 2. Reiki is a Japanese word for "universal life energy". It is based on the belief that unseen life force energy flows through every human being, animal, and object in the world. It is an alternative healing method that allows the body to heal itself naturally once the energy blocks are removed. It is not a religious practice and can never cause harm. A Reiki Master attunes a student's body with five Reiki symbols connecting them to universal energy allowing them to bring forth energy into their hands. A Reiki practitioner transmits this energy into a client's body with his/her hands in order to release physical, mental, and emotional blockages. As a result, the client experiences a feeling of peace and serenity.

While continuing to heal the wounds of my past, my therapy sessions became very emotional leaving me with stomach pain. After having a Reiki session, I noticed that the pain in my stomach had subsided. This is when I knew that I wanted to become a Reiki Master. Jane, a nurse friend, informed me of the American Holistic Nurses Association who offered a certification in holistic healing. We decided to get the information we needed, filled out our applications, and were both accepted into the Association. We drove to Massachusetts every weekend for three months to attend classes and learn about alternative therapies. We were each assigned a faculty advisor whom we were accountable to, and who gave us assignments to complete. We learned about therapies, such as stress management, Craniosacral treatment, Reiki, massage, Ayurvedic medicine, meditation, and therapeutic touch. One of my assignments was to write a spiritual story about myself. I wrote about how the journey in search of my true authentic self had become a lifelong adventure. As a child I never felt that I belonged to my family nor to this world. Instead I created a fantasy world where I felt safe. It was an inner energy force that drove me on a mission to search for that self.

After three months of classes, we spent another three months doing a practicum. I chose to do my practicum with David Mortimer who had a practice teaching stress management, mindful meditation and Ayurvedic medicine. Mindful meditation is a state of consciousness where the mind becomes tranquil and focused on the body's emotional and physical discomforts. Scanning the body from head to toe to identify sites of discomfort, taking a deep breath and releasing the discomfort with an exhalation helps to balance and heal the body/mind and emotions. I learned how to relax and reduce stress and anxiety by doing mindful meditation. Ayurvedic medicine originated in India and is a method of eating nutritional foods that are applicable to an individual's body type and reducing or avoiding foods that cause imbalance of the body/mind/

spirit. Adhering to the appropriate foods creates a natural flow of energy, fluids, oxygen, and nutrients to vital organs, tissues, cells, bone, muscle, and skin thus resulting in the elimination of toxic matter that accumulates in the body causing disease. The supplements and the nutritional guide of Ayurveda medicine has kept me healthy. Not only was this an exciting and healthy experience for Jane and I, but it also allowed us to meet several new nurse friends.

I chose to focus on Reiki while Jane chose to practice massage therapy. We both incorporated our knowledge of alternative healing methods in our nurse practice. Jane suggested that I start dating again. However, I was fearful of dating because I didn't know what men would expect of me. I was never intimate with any other man prior to my previous husband. I finally decided to join a dating service and met some men that I enjoyed spending time with. Unfortunately, I was attracted to men who were interesting and exciting but drank too much.

Believing that I needed to change myself before I continued on dating had me call Yolanda to have a session with her. She suggested that I needed to work on my codependency issues. Codependency is a learned behavior that can be passed down from one generation to another. It is an emotional and behavioral condition that affects an individual's ability to have a healthy, mutually satisfying relationship. It is also known as "relationship addiction" because people often form or maintain relationships that are one-sided, emotionally destructive and/or abusive. Co-dependency behavior is learnt by watching and imitating other family members who display this type of behavior. I had learnt this behavior from my mother. It was important for me to elevate and strengthen my self-esteem, self-empowerment, and self-worth in order to become independent. As such, I joined a co-dependency group to do this. I like being a part of a group because everyone learns from one another.

George, the facilitator of the Shaman group I participated in for two years, suggested that I take a Shamanic Journey with a female Shaman and Therapist he knew. A Shamanic Journey is a journey into the deepest part of one's inner life, which is not limited by learned belief systems. It is a place of possibilities, of creativity and of vision. The Shamanic Journey is also a way in which to recognize your true power, the power to live as an individual of integrity and authenticity. When I spoke to Janet, she told me that I would be staying at her home overnight, have meals there, journey in the east, south, west, and north sections of her two acres of land followed by counseling sessions. Stands Tall was my guide on the journey. I would write in my journal all day and share it with Janet. I also discussed family, grief, and personal issues with her. She did chair therapy where there was an empty chair and I would imagine the person that I have an issue with sitting in that chair. I would express my emotions to that person and Janet would in turn respond to me. It was a different type of therapy that relieved me of my grief, anger, and sadness. I slept in a tepee on her land that night while she drummed from her house. I became fearful when I discovered a slug in the tepee. I never saw a slug in my life and needed to ask Janet if it would harm me. She assured me that it wouldn't. When I awakened in the morning, I noticed a laser impression on the paper of my journal in the form of a buffalo. This experience bothered me until I shared it with Janet who informed me that spirit was informing me that the white buffalo was my power animal and would always protect me. I currently have a statue of a white buffalo in my home. That weekend experience overwhelmed me, so I shared it with George who informed me that my Shaman spirits were working with me. I completed Reiki 2 with Susan and began to practice on my friends and family. I received great feedback from my participants.

I finally decided that it was time for me to start dating again. I joined another dating company where I met Bob Betty. They had a profile and video tape of all their clients. Bob was a plumber who worked for Aetna Insurance Company, had a nice smile, and enjoyed outdoor activities. He said that he liked my looks, work history and my interest in outdoor activities. Our first date was at a fair with animals, arts, crafts, and lots of food. He always tells everyone that he decided to marry me because the smell of animals never bothered me. My mother raised chickens and I often gathered the eggs in the chicken coup which had that same smell. We discovered we were both raised in the country and were one hundred percent French. We went to a restaurant after the fair. I ordered a glass of wine and Bob ordered a club soda. I asked why he didn't order a drink of alcohol. He said that he was a recovering alcoholic with three years of sobriety. I thought, "If I could validate his statement by continuing to date him, he could possibly be the man that I would eventually marry". I did not want to marry a man with a drinking or drug problem again. After dating for six months, we decided to live in my condo to see if we were compatible. This arrangement would have never entered my mind if Bob had not talked about marriage. I didn't want to marry him without knowing if we could have a harmonious, loving, caring, and sharing relationship. One day while we were shopping in Mystic, we went into a gem store where I couldn't take my eyes off a simple hand-crafted ring with Tanzanite stones and diamonds. I couldn't afford to buy it, so Bob bought it for me. He liked a hand-crafted gold nugget ring at the same store which I bought for him on my credit card. After we left the store, we looked at each other and simultaneously said, "It looks like we got engaged". After that was said, I wanted to buy a dress for our wedding at my favorite store which was on the same street. We both laughed at our behavior and decided to visit a real estate office around the corner. Bob owned a boat and we wanted to buy a house near the ocean so we could get use out of the boat. Within three months, we bought a house in Old Lyme, Connecticut close to a lake. I grew up near a lake and always wanted to live near one again. We could launch Bob's boat in the lake, as well as in the ocean. We ended up with three mortgages until we sold our condominiums which took longer than anticipated because the market for condos at that time was poor. A lot of remodeling needed to be done on our new home, but Bob was a handy man and did most of it himself. We were happy, enjoyed our home and the town we lived in.

No matter where I lived, I was always blessed with someone walking into my life who would provide me with a new adventure. I met Kathy Valentine who was a Reiki teacher and Shaman. Kathy did some Reiki healing on me and became my teacher for Reiki 3 and for the Master level. After learning four levels of Reiki, I could now teach Reiki myself. Working with Kathy for two years made me realize that my creator was guiding me to be an energy healer. Bob didn't share my belief in energy healing but accepted my need to pursue starting my own Reiki practice.

In 1996, at the age of sixty-two, after living with Bob for two years, we decided to make wedding plans. Although we were both Catholic, we wanted our wedding to be unique, so we decided to have a Shaman wedding. We made plans to marry on May 30th and asked Kathy to perform the ceremony. She was not available, therefore her husband, Dale who was also a Shaman, performed the ceremony. We asked Bob's oldest brother, Donald, to be his best man. My son gave me away and my daughter was my maid-of-honor. My sister-in-law, Carroll Pugmire, along with seven of my best friends for over fifty years were my bridesmaids. They dressed as angels and recited their special message to us in a gazebo near the Connecticut River. Bob and I recited our marriage vows which we wrote together that stated that we pledged equality in decisions, goals, and life choices. Everyone who attended our wedding said they would never forget this unique ceremony. We had a breakfast brunch on a large boat while cruising the Connecticut River. After the cruise ended, we had another reception at our new senior citizens club. Appetizers were served by my seven angel bridesmaids whose names were, Ann Marie Delevieleuse, Rosalie Forte, Irene Picard, Beverly Middendorf, Dolores Pearl, Joan Lo Russo and Joan Gervasoni. We always had a special energy connection while raising our children, attending social events, playing golf, and traveling to places of interest. We danced at the reception, socialized, and had fun with everyone who had attended.

As a wedding gift, three couples who owned a condo in Myrtle Beach, Florida allowed us to stay at their condo for our honeymoon. This was Bob's first trip to Florida which made our honeymoon super special. We were grateful for the use of their condo which was decorative and enjoyable. The most memorable place we visited was Brook-Green Gardens which had the most comprehensive collection of American sculptures in the country. We saw some of the most beautiful sculptures and botanical gardens of our lifetime. We loved the warm weather, swimming in the ocean, and eating good food at the restaurants that our friends recommended.

Bob and I shared the same interests in nature, museums, traveling and socializing with friends and family. Upon returning from our honeymoon, we went back to work and bought a canoe to paddle in the lake, along with a motorcycle to cruise around Old Lyme and other areas of interest. We were very compatible and happy which was something I hadn't felt in a long time.

In October of 2000, I received a phone call from my nephew Scott informing me that my brother Raymond had died. Scott tried to help his father recover from alcoholism by getting him into a rehabilitation center and having him attend twelve-step meetings. Raymond continued to relapse and eventually Scott understood that he was powerless over his father's disease of alcoholism. Raymond was the brother who was my best friend during my childhood years. We had a great relationship and lots of fun together. Later in life I socialized with him and his family until his behavior, while under the influence of drugs and alcohol, became problematic. His wife eventually moved to Florida with her two other children. Scott remained in Connecticut. My brother Raymond was never the same after finding out that our father hung himself. He never would never discuss his emotions nor his abuse of alcohol and drugs with me. I believed that he had PTSD but would not seek treatment because he did not believe that counseling could help him. He died from the disease of alcoholism by himself with no loved ones by his side. I was devastated by the manner in which he died and was glad that my mother didn't have to witness yet another death in her family.

I resigned from my job at Blueridge Center and obtained a job at Rushford Center in Middletown which was closer to our home in Old Lyme. After working as a staff nurse on the detox unit for three months, my nursing supervisor asked me to create an admissions unit. I had never done this before but was honored to have been asked. I worked in the admissions unit for one year then decided to work as a counselor on the detox unit. In order to do this, I had to take a cut in pay and study to become an International Certified Alcohol and Drug Counselor. Four thousand hours of counseling experience was required along with an oral exam followed by a written exam. Working as a counselor in the detox unit was much different than working as a nurse. I worked sixty hours instead of forty like the counselors did at Blueridge Center. Comp time was also difficult to obtain. I liked interacting with our patients especially because I was able to help them make healthy lifestyle changes. Being able to impact my client's behavior and attitude towards the use of drugs and alcohol made me feel so good. I didn't get that same fulfillment when I was working as a nurse delivering medications to clients who were drug seekers and not open to using healthy coping skills. Their focus was instantaneous gratification. I felt more empowered and fulfilled working as a counselor. After working one year as a detox counselor, I was offered a job in the Outpatient Duel Diagnoses Program which I accepted after not getting comp time on the detox unit. I loved working with the program Psychiatrist who was a compassionate Doctor from India. We had an energy connection. He shared with me his spiritual beliefs and gave me some reading material which enabled me to have a whole different view of the world. He inspired me to write educational articles on mental illness which he reviewed. This was when I began my writing journey and knew I was being divinely guided in everything I wrote.

I began to think about retiring but needed to obtain more counseling hours before doing so. I cut my hours to part-time and worked as a Utilization Review Specialist on the detox unit for another year. I managed to get my four thousand hours and passed my oral and written exams. Before I retired, I decided to use the Employee Assistance Program since I hadn't grieved the death of my youngest brother Robert whom I helped my mother raise. I made an appointment with the counselor, wrote down all my issues, emotions, and thoughts about the death of all my brothers and presented them to her. She listened intently, offered me emotional support, and helped me finalize my grief process. It was good that I had made that decision because not long afterwards, Dolores, my angel friend who was in my wedding party informed me that she had breast cancer and was going to have a lumpectomy of her left breast. I couldn't digest what she had told me because we were both Holistic Nurses who lived a healthy lifestyle. We had been on a spiritual journey together for many years along with being in a meditation group at her home for ten years. Staying with her while she had the lumpectomy was emotionally painful for me. She used both alternative and medical treatments for over a year and then the cancer spread to her right breast. She chose not to have any further treatment. The thought of her dying was devastating. I told Bob that I wanted to retire because I was sixty-eight at that time and feared being diagnosed with the same fatal disease before having the opportunity to enjoy the retirement we had planned when Bob became sixty-five years old. Bob honored my emotional state of being and sent in his resignation. We both had retirement parties and prayed that we didn't make a mistake in retiring early. We bought a thirty-foot Cedar Creek fifth wheel motor home to hook up to our new truck. We planned to travel to several places in the United States and Canada. We sold our home when real estate market was very high. The first person who was interested in it, bought it for the price we wanted because all of the remodeling we did, along with the furniture. We felt very fortunate to have sold our home so fast.

In 2002, we started on our trip throughout Canada. Our first stop was Prince Edward Island where we stayed at a campsite. Meeting new people from all over the country at campsites was entertaining. We continued on our journey visiting Montreal, Quebec City, and the Providence of Quebec where we visited my mother's family. I never shared our family's history with my relatives because my mother kept it a secret from them. We enjoyed our visit and continued on to visit Gaspe where we saw the famous Perce Rock which is a huge sheer formation in the Gulf of Saint Laurence on the tip of Gaspe Peninsula in Quebec. It is the world's largest natural arch with a huge hole in its middle. We love the natural formations of nature. While we were on this trip, I received a phone call informing me that Dolores had died. Although I had kept in touch with her while traveling, I felt guilty because I couldn't be there for her before she died. Dolores painted beautiful portraits and scenery pictures. I bought a pastel picture of a sailboat she had painted which currently hangs on my dining room wall. Whenever I look at it, I think of her.

In 2005, after traveling in our fifth wheel for four years, we decided to buy a condo in Florida. We visited my sister-in-law who owned a condo in Fort Pierce, Florida. After selling our fifth wheel and truck, we bought a new car, truck, and condo near my sister-in-law. Bob got a part time job as maintenance man in our condo complex and I got a part time job at New Horizons of the Treasure Coast on the psychiatric unit for four years before being transferred to the detox unit where I continued to work as a per diem staff nurse. My nursing supervisor Donna Molnar is a compassionate person who holds her staff accountable for their work.

We decorated and remodeled our new home. We loved the feeling of living in the comfort of five rooms instead of the two rooms of our fifth wheel. We had also bought a park model home in Rhode Island in Timber Creek RV park where we stayed while traveling in our fifth wheel. We made several friends in this RV park which was two hours away from where my children, friends and relatives lived in Connecticut. After four years of traveling back and forth from Florida, we sold the park model and remained permanently in Florida except for occasionally visiting our family and friends in Connecticut.

Jack, my ex-husband, bought a home in Ocala, Florida and lived there with his significant other whose name was Rose. Once I released my anger and grief over Jack's behavior, I was able to forgive him and have a relationship with him and Rose. This made my children feel good and we were able to enjoy our family times together. I couldn't find anyone in Fort Pierce who knew about Reiki or thought about spirituality the way I did. After doing some research, I found Spark of Divine Healing and Learning Center in Vero Beach, about an hour away from Fort Pierce. The owner, Beth Franks, informed me about all the activities she had. Metaphysical books, Reiki, yoga, massage, and spiritual classes were available. I felt as though I discovered a goldmine as I could participate in all my favorite activities. I was excited to meet new friends with whom I could share my thoughts and beliefs. I attended a Shaman presentation in 2012 by Debra Willow Fire Woman and felt the same energy connection as I did with all the other Shamans who entered my life. After having a shamanic healing session with Debra, she asked me if I would like to participate in her Shaman group. I agreed and ended up attending her Shaman classes on weekends for two years. Shamans work from the perspective that matter and humans are connected to the energy of the universe. It is one of the oldest healing traditions of indigenous people and cultures. A Shaman teacher uses the Munay-Ki-Harmony Rite to instill seven archetypes (power animals) into each of the students seven chakras as seeds to grow and gain power energy. A shaman practitioner has the ability to transform and heal the conflicts between body, mind and spirit created by the chaotic pace of modern life. He/she heals what is energetically out of balance so that physical, psychological and/or emotional problems do not manifest. After having several healing treatments with Debra, positive changes in my physical and emotional well-being were apparent. I felt connected to universal energy and became aware of an elevation in my consciousness. When we had our graduation ceremony, Debra said that we would receive a gift from the universe. The next morning Bob came home with a crystal stone eleven inches wide and sixteen inches long with over sixty crystals on it. He told me that he found it on the ground near the dumpster. He asked the grounds keeper how it got there, and he said that he didn't know, although it wasn't there the previous day. He asked the grounds keeper if he could take it home to his wife who loves crystals. I was ecstatic when he brought it home. I knew the universe had sent it to me as Debra mentioned. I read several books about crystals and their healing energy. The reason why crystals and gemstones are beautiful, mystical, and profound "energy medicine tools" is due to what science calls their piezoelectric effect. Crystals and gemstones respond to the electricity that is coursing throughout our bodies and if we are sluggish, constant electrical vibrations of the stones will help harmonize, balance, and stimulate these energies. I have crystals placed throughout my house for energy protection. I place positive affirmations under my small crystals and on top of my large crystal to manifest my affirmation. Sometimes certain events need to occur before they can manifest but eventually, they do manifest. An affirmation is a mental or verbal declaration to yourself and to the universe about what you need or desire out of life such as, "I will receive the money needed to buy a home".

I met Kitty Elder at Spark of Divine who is a teacher, Reiki Master, Shaman practitioner and photographer. I used her photo for my book cover of " Creating a Wholesome Human Being". She educates the public about crystals, their properties, and the spiritual energy they give off. To this day, we are still friends.

I also met Patricia Condi at Spark of Divine Healing Center who is a retired teacher, student counselor, Reiki Master and Shaman. We got together to create a woman's empowerment group which we facilitated for one year. We charged fifteen dollars for one session a week. Our focus was on elevating self-esteem and self-worth with the intention of empowering the six women in our group. We gave homework assignments to help them identify negative thoughts, irrational beliefs, emotional distress, and self-defeating behaviors. These women thanked us for helping them make healthy changes. Because we received great feedback from our clients and the owner of the facility, we decided to create grief and inner child groups. These groups were also successful. Patricia and I enjoyed watching members of our groups grow in consciousness.

I began to focus on developing my own practice called "Source Healing" in which I used a holistic approach to uncover core issues that prevented physical, emotional, and mental wellness. When I perform any healing, my focus is on the chakras which are the seven energy centers in the body that start at the coccyx bone and reach up along the spinal cord to the top of the head. Chakras are shaped like a wheel and have specific colors. A healthy chakra is one that spins rapidly in a clockwise direction with no blockage in the flow of body energy. Chakras that are blocked will spin counterclockwise and can cause mental and physical illnesses. Shaman/Reiki energy brought forth by the practitioner will release and clear any blockages in the chakras that interfere with wellness. The first chakra is the root chakra located at the base of the spine and is the color red. It governs the health of the spine, colon, and rectum. When it is balanced, one will feel grounded to mother earth. The second chakra is the sacral chakra located below the naval and is the color orange. It governs the health of the ovaries, womb, prostate and genitals. When it is balanced, one will feel sexually adequate. The third chakra is the solar plexus located above the naval and is the color yellow. It governs the pancreas, stomach liver and intestines. When it is balanced, one will feel a sense of empowerment. The fourth chakra is the heart chakra located in the center of the chest and is the color blue. It governs the heart, lungs, and circulation. When it is balanced, one will feel unconditional love of self and others. The fifth chakra is the throat chakra located in the throat and is the color blue. When it is balanced, one will have no issues speaking their truth. The sixth chakra is the third eye located between the eyebrows and is the color indigo. It governs the health of pituitary, gland, throat, and mouth. When it is balanced, one will have insight and intuitiveness. The seventh chakra is the crown chakra located at the top of the head and is the color violet. It governs the pineal gland, cerebral cortex, skin, and eyes. When it is balanced, one's mind is alert and calm. When a practitioner is not able to release a specific blockage in an area of discomfort, she/he will refer the client to their doctor. A Reiki/Shaman practitioner never diagnoses a client.

My new friends introduced me to Meetup which is a service used to organize online groups that host in-person and virtual events for people with similar interest. I like to golf, do yoga and walk, write, swim, and attend theater shows. Meetup has groups that have all those activities which I love. One night, I met Grace Vergis at a professional networking event. Grace is a successful Life Navigator. We had an instantaneous energetic connection, therefore we decided to have lunch to get to know one another better. We discovered that we had energy healing in common and developed two workshops "Intuitive Energy Healers" and "Embracing a Unique Healing Modality". Through trial and error, we discovered that many people either aren't interested in alternative healing treatments or don't have money to participate because insurance companies will not cover holistic treatment. In my thirty years of working with alcohol, drug, and mental illness, I noticed clients wanting a quick fix with medications from which they become addicted. Most clients were not receptive to healthy coping skills because their attention span was limited, and they only wanted to take a pill to feel better. This part of my work has been disappointing to me. A detox program in Connecticut trained nurses to do acupuncture in the ear lobe along with detox teas to detox the patients. Acupuncture needles were placed in specific areas of the ear lobe to help the body heal itself, to keep the patients calm, reducing cravings and withdrawal symptoms. As a result, the patients experienced a safe and comfortable detox process, but the insurance companies would not pay for this type of treatment. They would only cover payment for drugs which the patients are trying to detox from. Grace introduced me to Amonda-Rose Igoe who spent eight hours educating me on formulating and delivering presentations. She is also known as "The Speaking Goddess" who instilled the confidence I needed to deliver presentations. Grace also introduced me to Dr. Kim Potter who is a Behavioral Scientist. He developed the Blueprint for Changes Program which teaches people about behaviorism and why they behave consistently the way they do. I learned to focus on behavior and evaluate the mental beliefs and emotional core of behavior. I pray for the day when the government and insurance companies recognize the benefit of integrating the medical model with alternative therapies in the field of chemical dependency and mental health.

A client of mine introduced me to Prudy Buchl who facilitated a Reiki/Shaman healing group at her home. It was five minutes from my home, so I no longer had to venture out to Vero Beach. We met once a week with other Reiki Masters to heal one other.

As I am finishing writing this chapter, I heard the phone ring and when I answered it, my sister-in-law informed me that my brother Jules had just died. He had been struggling with the disease of Leukemia for one year. I was sad and angry that COVID-19 had prevented me from being with him in his last days. He lived in Texas but also owned a condo in Florida. Over the years, we would spend quality time together having lunches, golfing, and playing pool. Whenever I made the attempt to talk about our past, Jules would automatically change the topic. Denying and suppressing his emotions helped him forget the past traumas we experienced, but it impacted his behavior and overall wellbeing. I will really miss interacting with him.

CHAPTER 7

From Caterpillar to Butterfly

I spent much of my childhood walking in the woods and sitting on a granite rock meditating to relax and get away from my dysfunctional family. I would watch caterpillars hanging upside down from a leaf with a silky cocoon surrounding it. I became mesmerized by this and thought to myself: "Wouldn't it be nice if I could be surrounded by a cocoon to protect myself from the all the pain I have to endure daily in my dysfunctional home". There is such a parallel between the transition of a caterpillar to a butterfly and my transition from a traumatized broken child to a fully healed transformed woman.

Along my journey, at my place of employment, I was given me a chrysalis to take home to my new condominium. I placed it in one of my plants and totally forgot about it, until one morning when I awoke and saw a Monarch butterfly flying around my room. That was one of the most memorable moments of my life.

In my practice "Source Healing" which takes a holistic approach to uncover core issues preventing physical and mental wellness, I use Rational Emotive Therapy. It is based on the premise that whenever a person becomes upset, it is not the event taking place that upsets us; it is the beliefs learnt from parents, educators, peers, family members and people in authority and religious educators that trigger emotional and behavioral responses to that event. Two people can view the same event and perceive it totally differently according to their subconscious limited beliefs. Positive changes occur once the layers of pretense are peeled away allowing one to discover the missing pieces to one's authenticity.

On my journey to become a transformed woman, I learned how to identify negative thoughts, irrational and self-defeating beliefs, as well as repressed emotions, and the impact each had on my behavior. I identified twelve irrational beliefs and spent a year focusing on changing them. I also had several negative thoughts that I needed to change. Once I completed this inner work, I noticed that my emotional reactions to events and my self-defeating behavior began to change for the better.

Our greatest challenge is never about what other people do, but rather about how we emotionally react, and respond to their actions. Spiritual growth is not about changing the world. It is about going within and changing oneself.

I have been fully transparent in this book. My goal is to help others learn and heal their lives through my painful experiences and journey to wellness. I would like to give my readers a sense of hope for the future, especially if they feel helpless, hopeless, and powerless. I want to show them that, they too, can recover from any trauma related incidences in their lives. I believe that my Creator put me on this earth to experience life's journey, learn how to heal my wounds, and in turn share everything I've learnt with others so that they can heal fully and be transformed into the beautiful butterfly they were destined to be. Lastly, I believe that my friends, teachers, and husbands were also placed in my life to help me learn my lessons, support me, and give me the love I so desperately craved.

CPSIA information can be obtained
at www.ICGtesting.com
Printed in the USA
LVHW090311170222
711378LV00003B/122

9 781954 341296